YOUR KNOWLEDGE HAS VALUE

- We will publish your bachelor's and
  master's thesis, essays and papers

- Your own eBook and book -
  sold worldwide in all relevant shops

- Earn money with each sale

Upload your text at www.GRIN.com
and publish for free

Anne-Mareike Franz

The women's suffrage movement in New Zealand

GRIN Verlag

Bibliografische Information der Deutschen Nationalbibliothek:

Die Deutsche Bibliothek verzeichnet diese Publikation in der Deutschen National-
bibliografie; detaillierte bibliografische Daten sind im Internet über http://dnb.d-
nb.de/ abrufbar.

Imprint:

Copyright © 2006 GRIN Verlag GmbH
Druck und Bindung: Books on Demand GmbH, Norderstedt Germany
ISBN: 978-3-656-56766-0

The Women's Suffrage Movement in New Zealand

On 19 September 1893 New Zealand became the first state in the world, which granted women the vote[1]. At this time Kate Sheppard, who was of great importance for the feminist movement, perceived the feelings of women in New Zealand as follows: "The General Elections have come and gone. For the first time the women of New Zealand have joined with men in choosing members of Parliament, and we have waited with bated breath for the deluge of calamities which it was prognosticated would follow the admission of women into the political arena."[2]Although this step seemed to be revolutionary and sudden considering the restricted political rights of women in many other countries, the development of the women's suffrage movement in New Zealand was without violence and the outcome of a long historical process[3].

The idea of the women's suffrage campaign was not initiated in New Zealand, but was influenced from earlier suffrage movements in Great Britain and in the United States, although this would be obvious for a country, which granted women the vote at first. In Great Britain, Mary Wollstonecraft set the first impulses with her work *A vindication of the rights of woman* (1792) arguing for equal rights and education. After her, the British philosopher and economist John Stuart Mill, who was very engaged in the suffrage movement, published in 1869 *On the subjection of women* about the feminist case, which achieved the spreading of the debate to the British colonies, Australia and New Zealand. Even before the suffrage movement in Great Britain started, the first convention for women's rights took place at Seneca Falls in 1848, where the American campaign was raised.[4] The "Woman's Christian Temperance Union" (WCTU) was founded in 1874 as a mouthpiece for this campaign, which aimed to achieve social reforms. As a consequence, the developments in Great Britain and in the United States both encouraged and influenced the suffrage movement in New Zealand[5].

---

[1] See Michael King, *The Penguin History of New* Zealand (Albany, Auckland: Penguin Books Ltd, 2003), p.265.
[2] http://www.teara.govt.nz/1966/W/WomensSuffrageMovement/WomensSuffrageMovement/en, 01.02.2006.
[3] See Tom Brooking, Paul Enright, *Milestones-Turning Points in NZ History* (Lower Hutt: Mills Publication, 1988), p.102.
[4] See http://www.nzine.co.nz/features/suffrage2.html, 01.02.2006.
[5] See http://www.nzhistory.net.nz/Gallery/Suffragists/SuffIntro.htm, 01.02.2006.

Following these examples early attempts at legislation started in New Zealand around 1870 at a time when women were classed politically with "juveniles, lunatics and criminals"[6]. Mary Ann Müller's published writings under the pseudonym "Femina'", which persuaded the important politicians William Fox and Alfred Saunders for example, can be seen as the beginning of New Zealand suffrage movement. In the same decade, Mary Colclough was in lively correspondence with the local press under the name "Polly Plum" supporting the ideas of Mill. As a consequence of the growing support for the suffragette movement, women in all provinces who owned property and paid taxes where allowed to vote in municipal elections in 1875. After another success in 1894 women achieved the right to have their own property. Nevertheless Electoral Bills which sought to grant women ratepayers the vote for the Parliament failed in 1878, 1879, 1887. After this the question of parliamentary enfranchisement for women was set aside until the end of the decade, as it was doomed to fail in Parliament each time.[7]

But not only members of the Parliament were politically active at that time, as many women started to take action in public communities. In 1985 Mary Leavitt, a member of the WCTU in the United States, founded, with the assistance of Anne Ward branches of a organisation called "New Zealand Women's Christian Temperance Union" in Auckland. New members were easy to convince as both societies, in the United States and in New Zealand, had to deal with the same social problems in their countries, the abuse of alcohol for example.[8] Therefore members of the WCTU in New Zealand promoted enfranchisement of women to support legislation banning alcohol through their vote.[9] They also ran soup kitchens, did youth work and visited prisons and hospitals. In 1887 Kate Sheppard, a Christian socialist, became the leader of the WCTU and had great success through writing letters to the press, speeches, articles in the *Prohibitionist* and contact with politicians. Connections with the members of Parliament and their support were indeed an important instrument for the women in the WCTU. They convinced key members of the ministry like John Hall, John Ballance and John Vogel to become supporters for the suffrage movement. Nevertheless women were not successful in convincing the majority in Parliament for the enfranchisement at this stage.[10]

---

[6] Michael King,, p.264.
[7] See http://www.nzhistory.net.nz/Gallery/Suffragists/SuffIntro.htm, 01.02.2006.
[8] See http://www.nzhistory.net.nz/Gallery/Suffragists/SuffIntro.htm, 01.02.2006.
[9] See http://www.nzine.co.nz/features/suffrage2.html, 01.02.2006.
[10] See http://www.nzhistory.net.nz/Gallery/Suffragists/SuffIntro.htm, 01.02.2006.

This unsatisfying situation changed when the women's suffrage movement "gained momentum"[11] between 1890 and 1893. The WCTU now tried to reach "non-temperance women, working-class women, the educated elite, and women in more isolated areas"[12] with their message to collect names for suffrage petitions. After the first "Women's Franchise League" was initiated by Nicol, Morison and Hatton in 1892, the number of these organisations grew steadily and they often filled the gaps in regions where the WCTU was not active. Although the franchise leagues had no temperance connection, they were supported by the WCTU. But still the opposition, which was represented by the liquor industry and some members of the Parliament (e.g. Henry Smith Fish), was strong and active. Some of them even feared of the reversal of roles, the disempowerment of the husband by his wife at home, women as a radical force or conservative burden, if they were allowed to participate in politics. As a consequence the Electoral Bills, which passed the House of Representatives in 1891 and 1892, failed in the Legislative Council, which was more conservative. In 1893 the situation of enfranchisement got worse as John Ballance, who favoured women's suffrage, died and Richard John Seddon, who disliked this movement, became the new premier. Against the fears of the suffragists a new Women's Suffrage Bill was introduced and passed through the lower house with the help of John Hall and a women's petition of about 32,000 names. As the number of members in the upper house, who were for and against this bill, was evenly divided, the women and Seddon began to fight for their votes. The "Auckland Franchise League" sent white camellias to the supporters and the "Anti-Women's Franchise League" in Wellington sent red camellias to the opponents. As Seddon tried to force a member to vote against the bill, two changed their mind and voted for it. With the result of 20 to 18 the bill passed on 8 September and was signed by the governor on 19 September, although opponents still tried to convince him not to do so.[13] In November women in New Zealand were allowed to vote for the new Parliament, which seemed to be the fulfilment of their efforts in the enfranchisement campaign.[14]

Nevertheless it seems reasonable to ask whether this outcome of the suffragette movement meant a change for the women in New Zealand or not. Considering the results of their voting on the one hand, many just voted the same candidates as their husbands or fathers. Women still had to face discrimination between the sexes in choosing a job and still tended to enter the workforce and rather than the professions. But on the other hand these

---

[11] http://www.nzhistory.net.nz/Gallery/Suffragists/SuffIntro.htm, 01.02.2006.
[12] http://www.nzhistory.net.nz/Gallery/Suffragists/SuffIntro.htm, 01.02.2006.
[13] See http://www.nzhistory.net.nz/Gallery/Suffragists/SuffIntro.htm, 01.02.2006.
[14] See http://www.nzine.co.nz/features/suffrage2.html, 01.02.2006.

women had only little goals like the enfranchisement or the right of property and they finally managed to vote and to make their life a little bit more comfortable. This was not the end of this process towards equality, it was only the start, which showed that these women could achieve something. So the consequences of the suffragette movement not only for New Zealand, but even more for other countries have to be taken into consideration. Although the women in New Zealand made only little steps, they encouraged other countries as a good example to follow. With regard to this later development we can say that at this time women in New Zealand definitely achieved a change of their of their situation, at least in their minds.[15]

In conclusion, the suffragette movement in New Zealand was a matter of both the work of the women and the supporting politicians and it had to face a long historical development, because of its revolutionary nature. Nevertheless today's society can't be imagined without these political achievements. In my opinion this quotation from André Siegfried states this thought the best: "That which in 1893 was regarded as slightly ridiculous is now treated as a very natural state of things, and no one is surprised to find women voting, making speeches, in a word, taking their part as citizens in public affairs. It can therefore be said that the feminist movement has left the heroic age and is now in the era of slow and practical realities."[16]

Sources:

King, Michael. *The Penguin History of New* Zealand. Albany, Auckland: Penguin Books Ltd, 2003.
Brooking, Tom; Enright, Paul. *Milestones-Turning Points in NZ History*. Lower Hutt: Mills Publication, 1988.
http://www.teara.govt.nz/1966/W/WomensSuffrageMovement/WomensSuffrageMovement/en, 01.02.2006.
http://www.nzine.co.nz/features/suffrage2.html, 01.02.2006.
http://www.nzhistory.net.nz/Gallery/Suffragists/SuffIntro.htm, 01.02.2006.

---

[15] See Tom Brooking, Paul Enright, pp.106/107.
[16] Tom Brooking, Paul Enright, p.107.